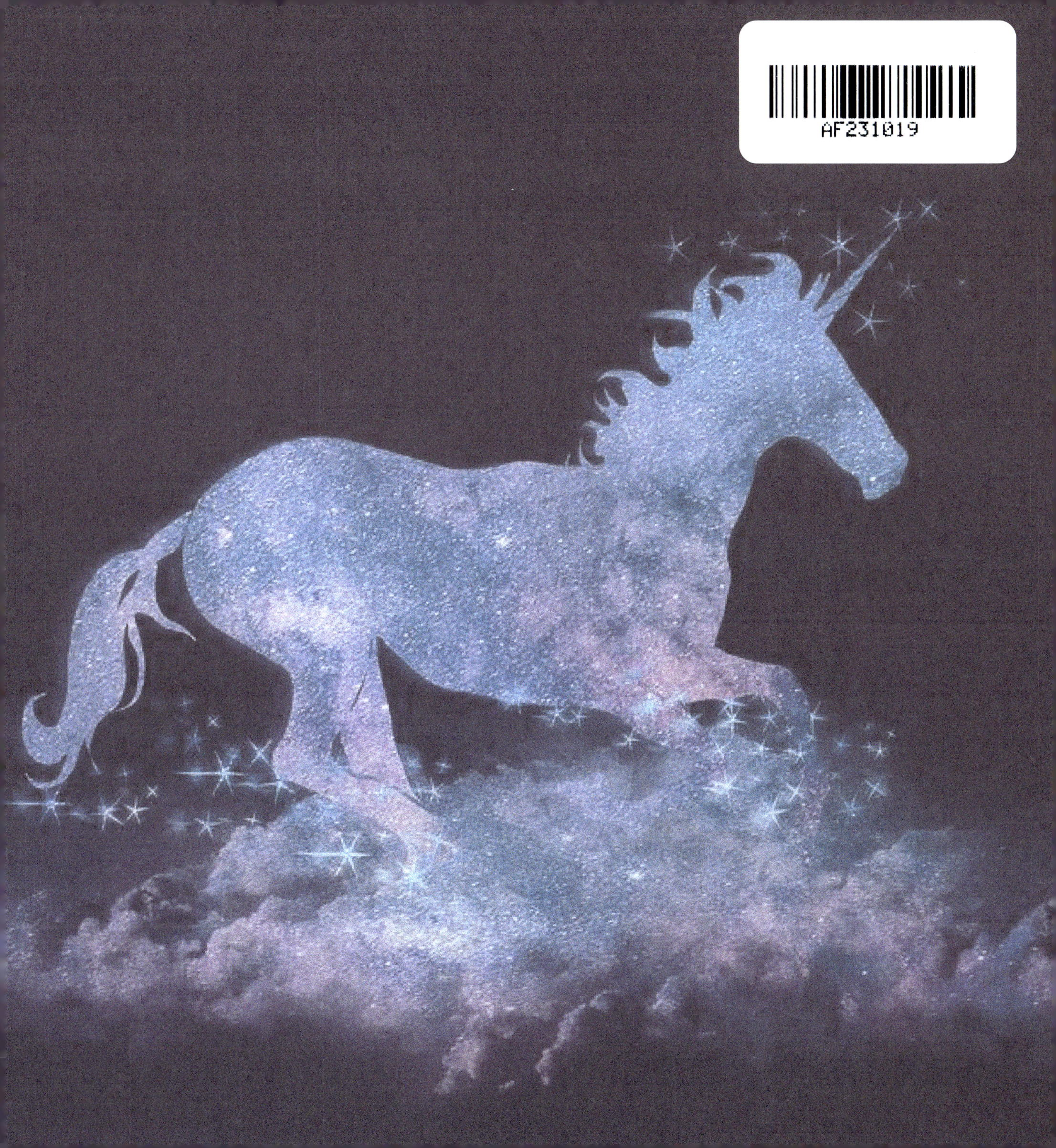

AF231019

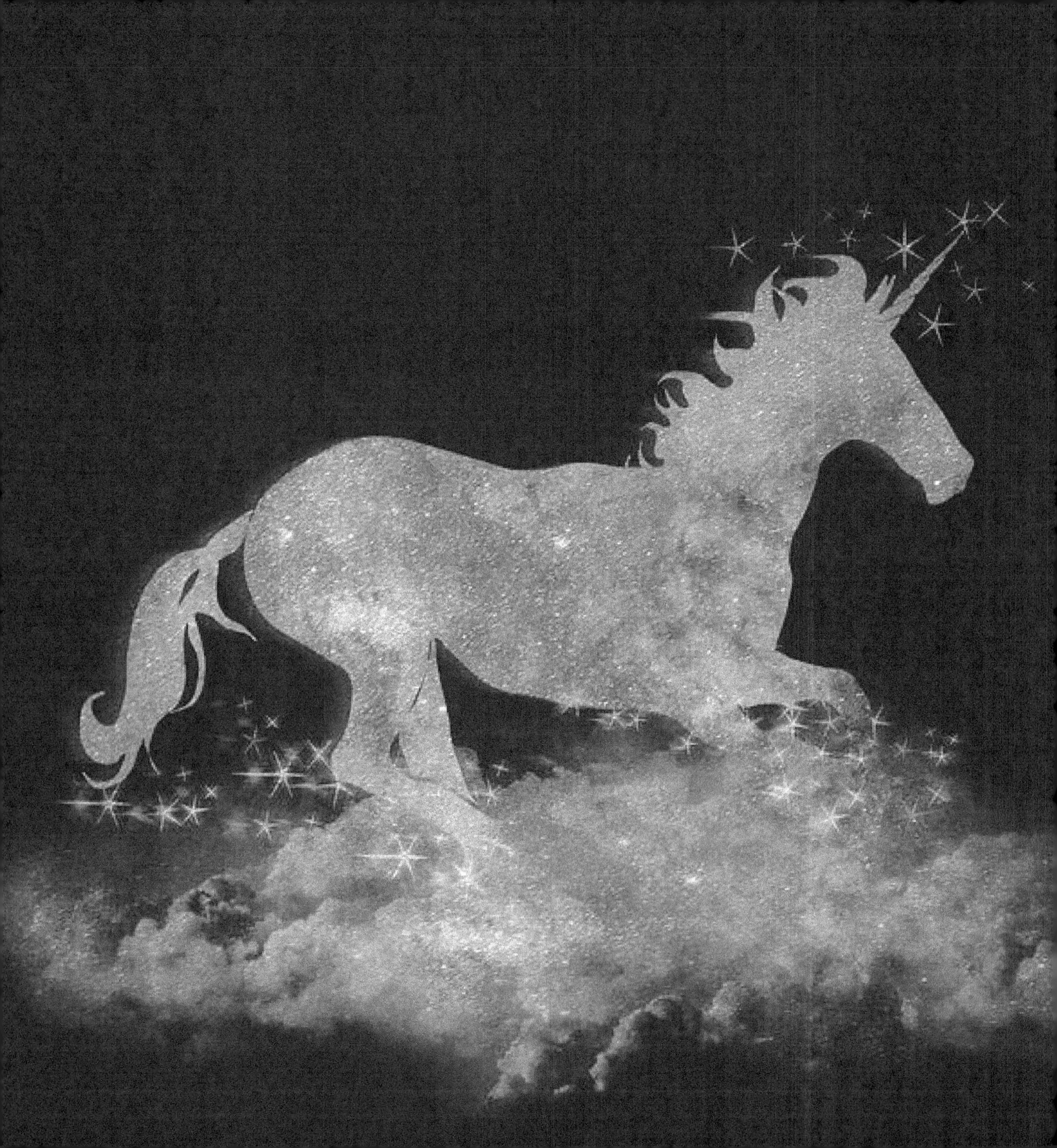

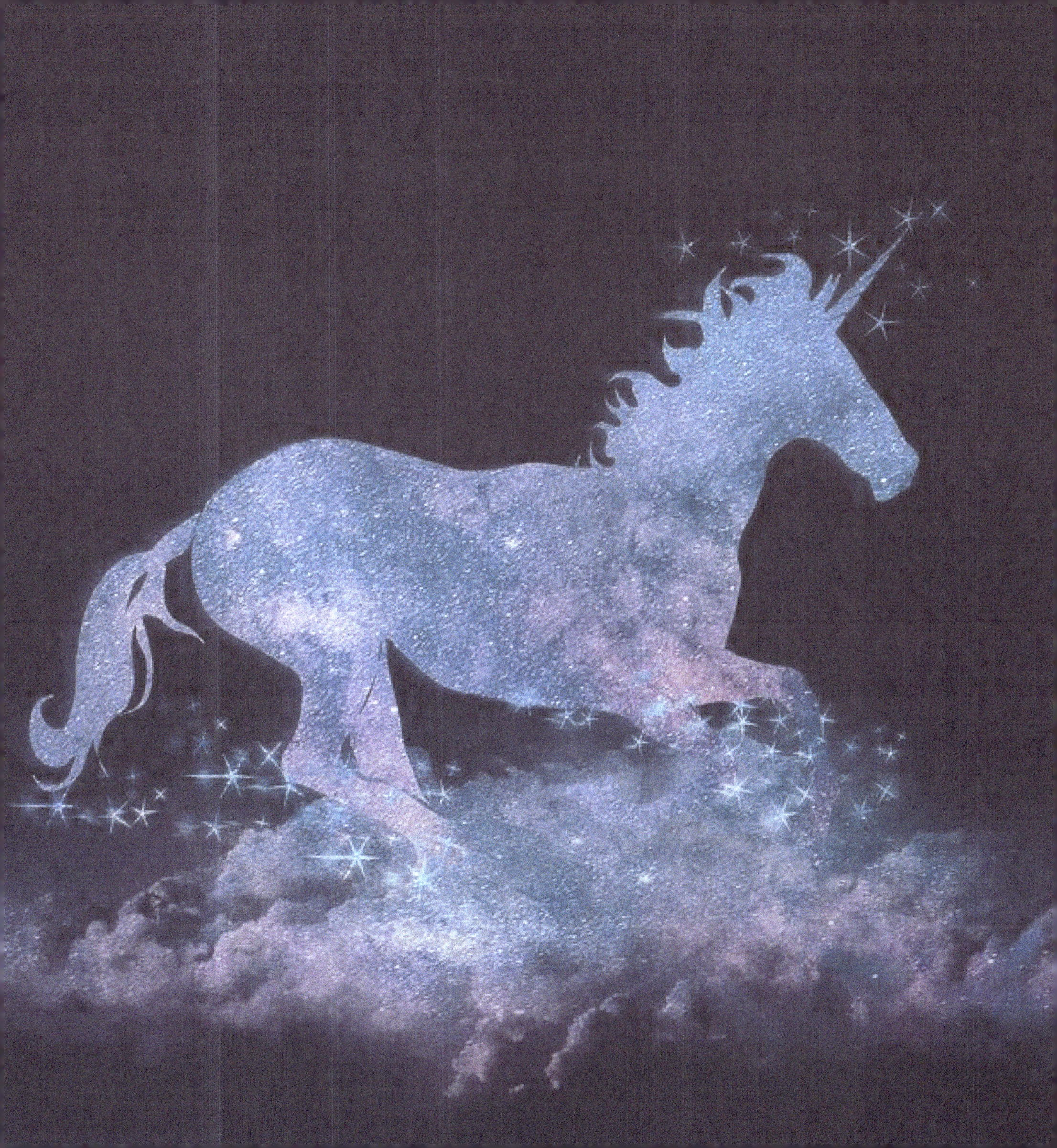

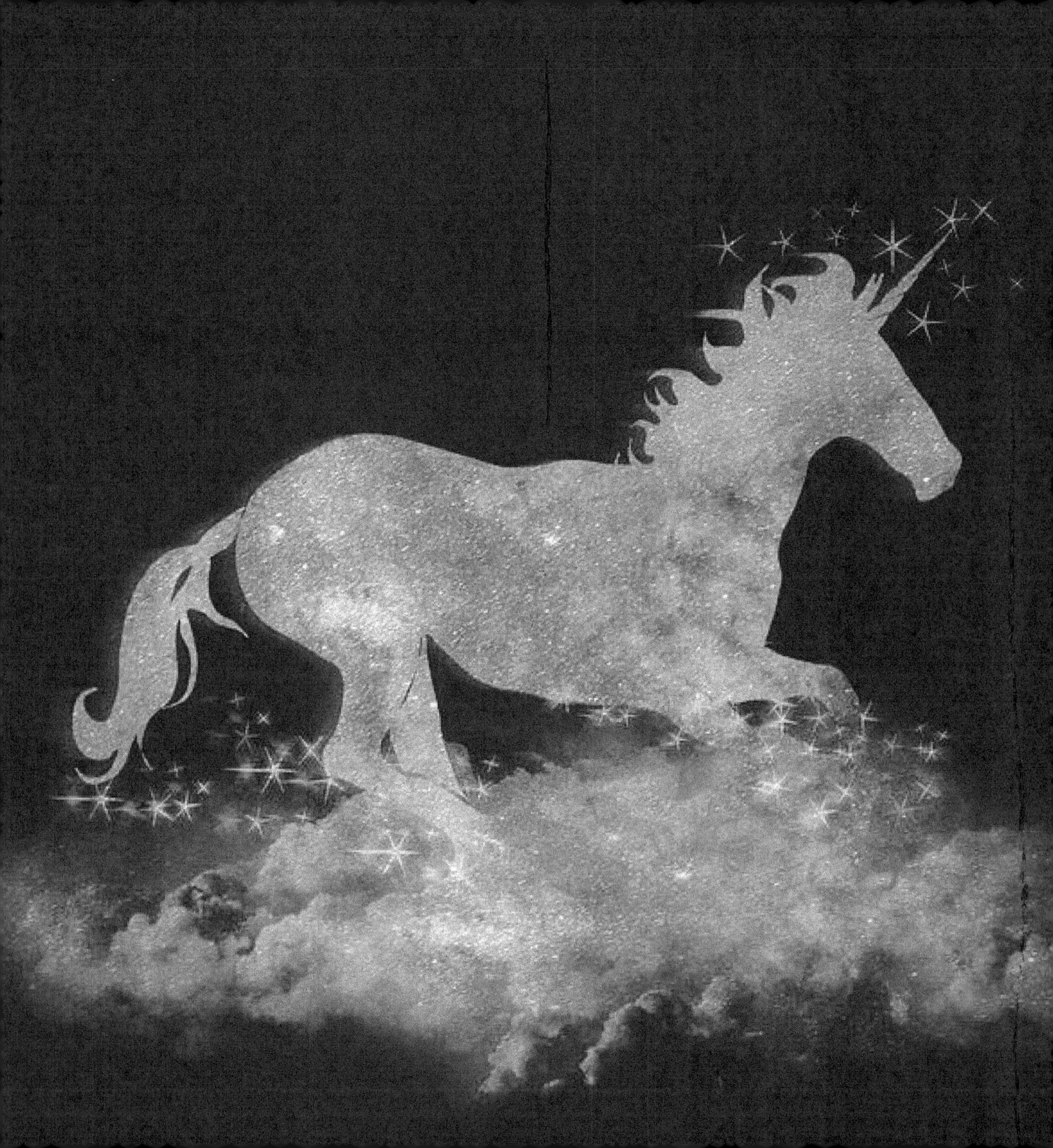

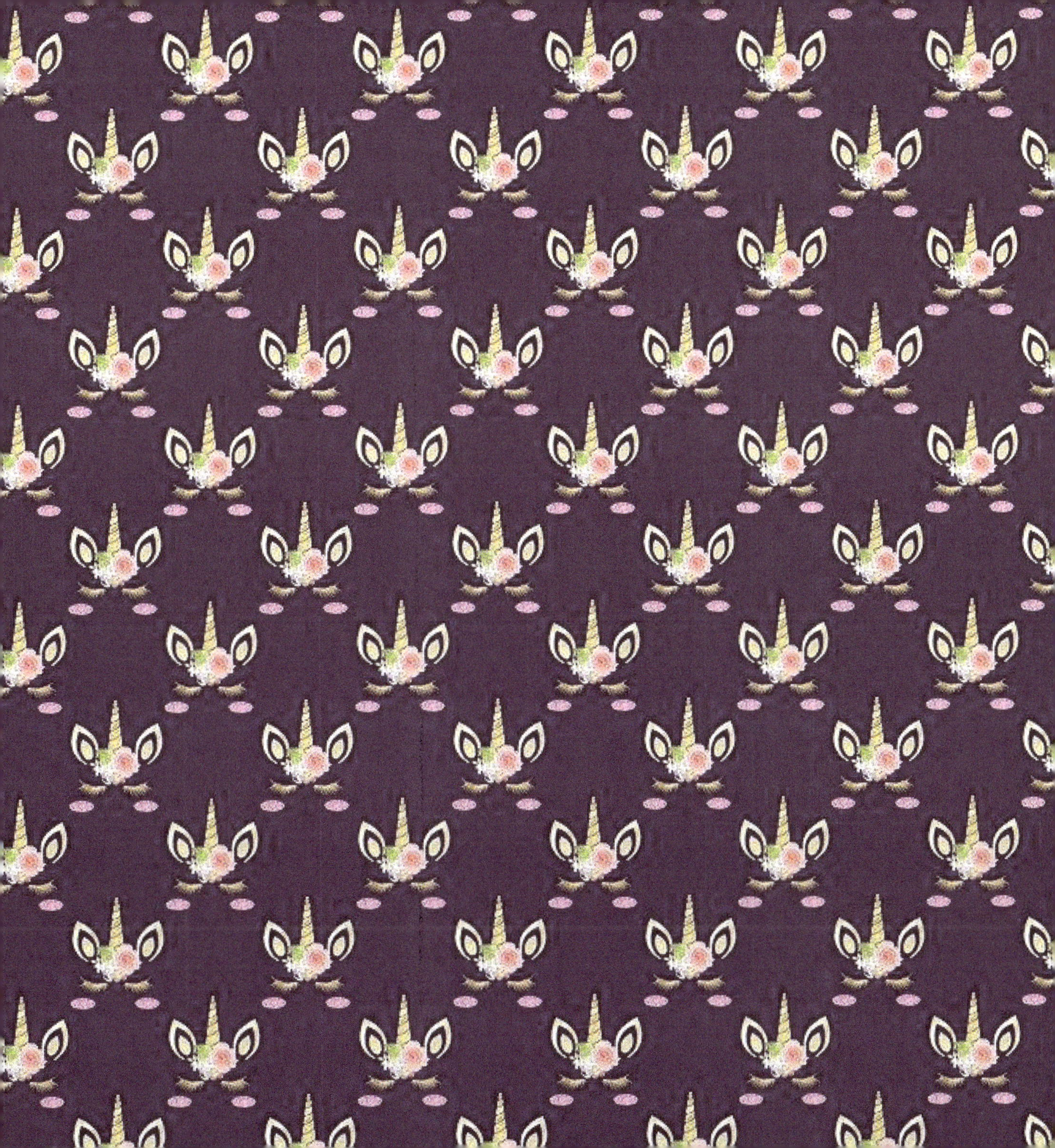

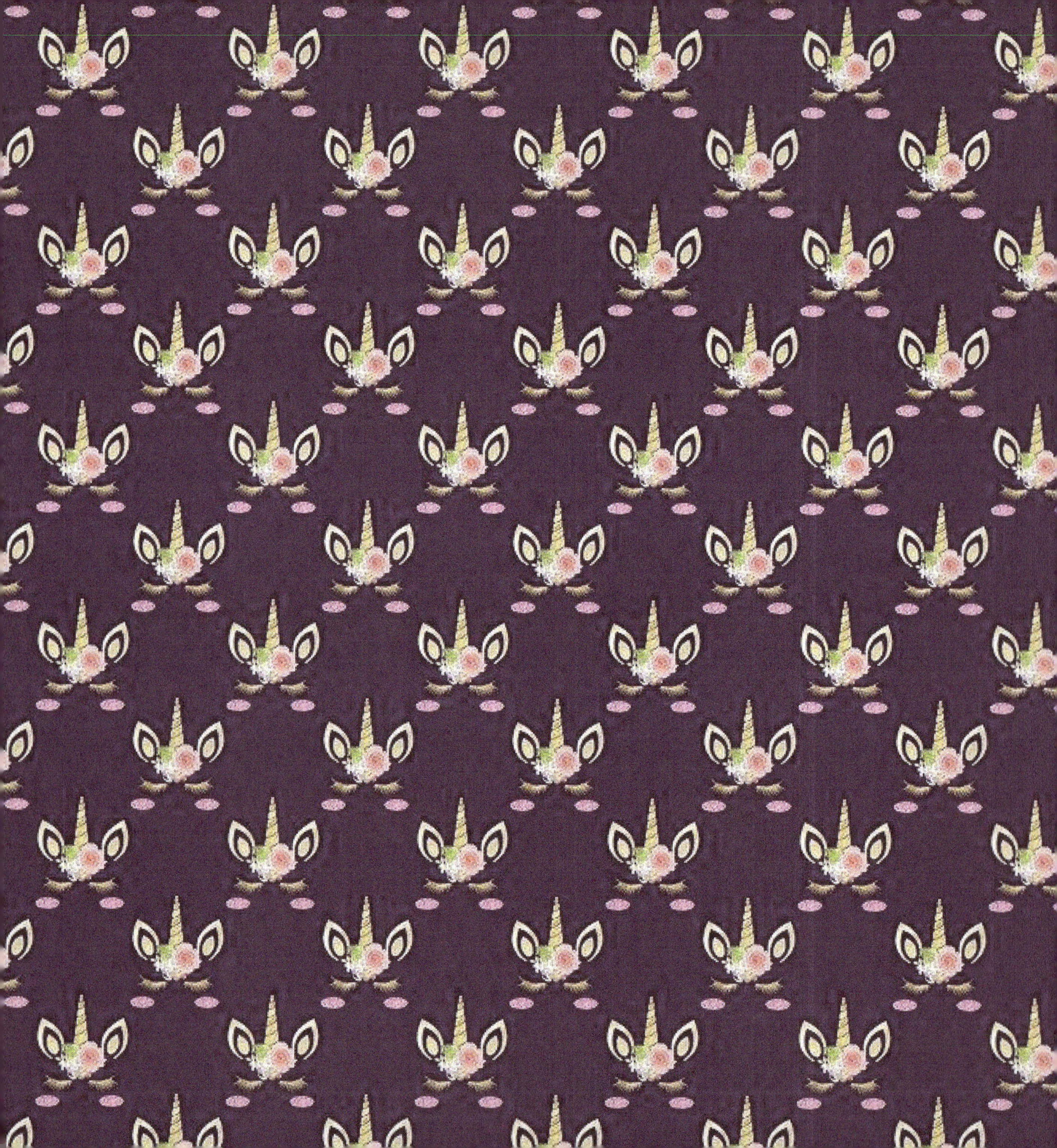

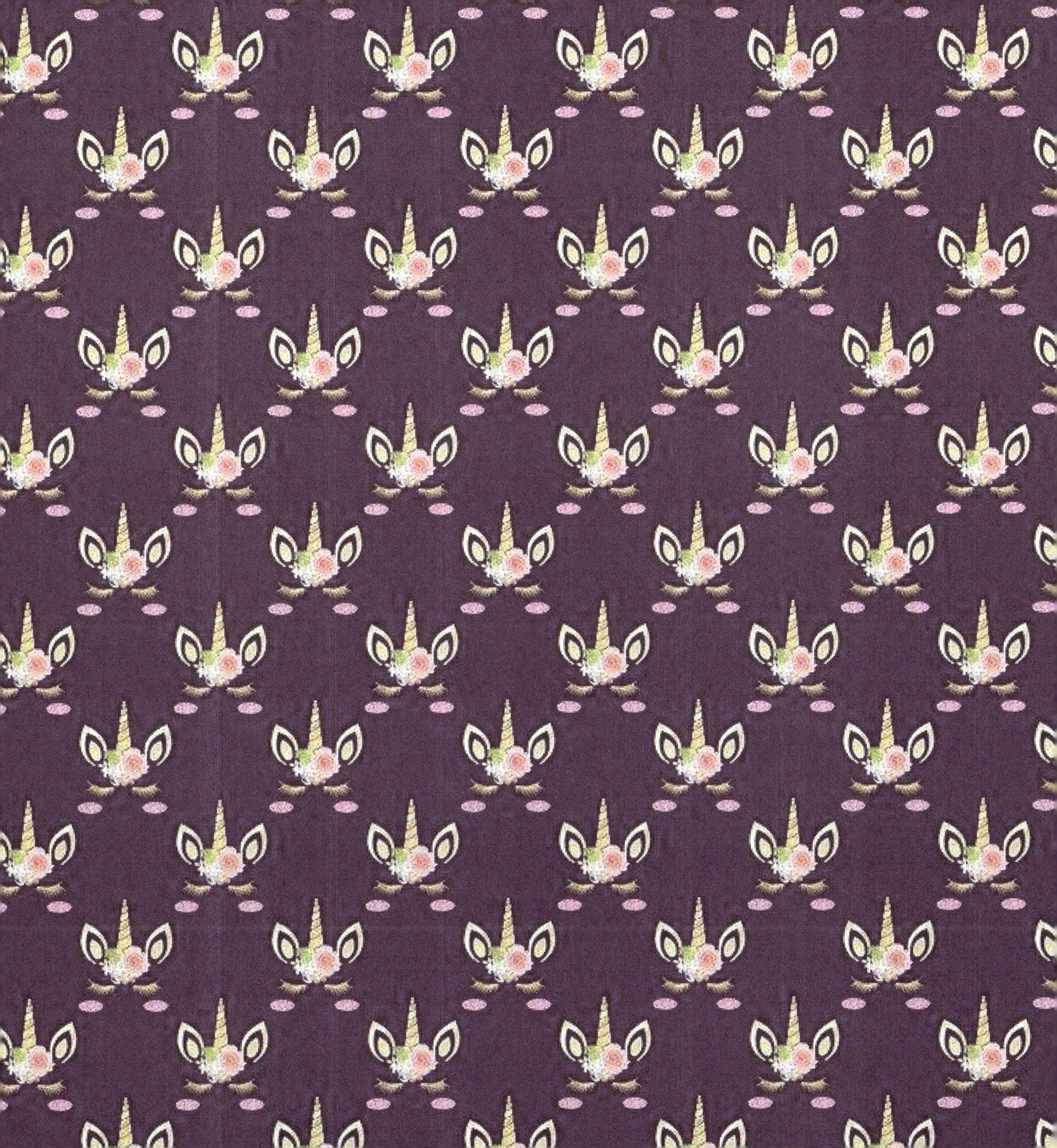

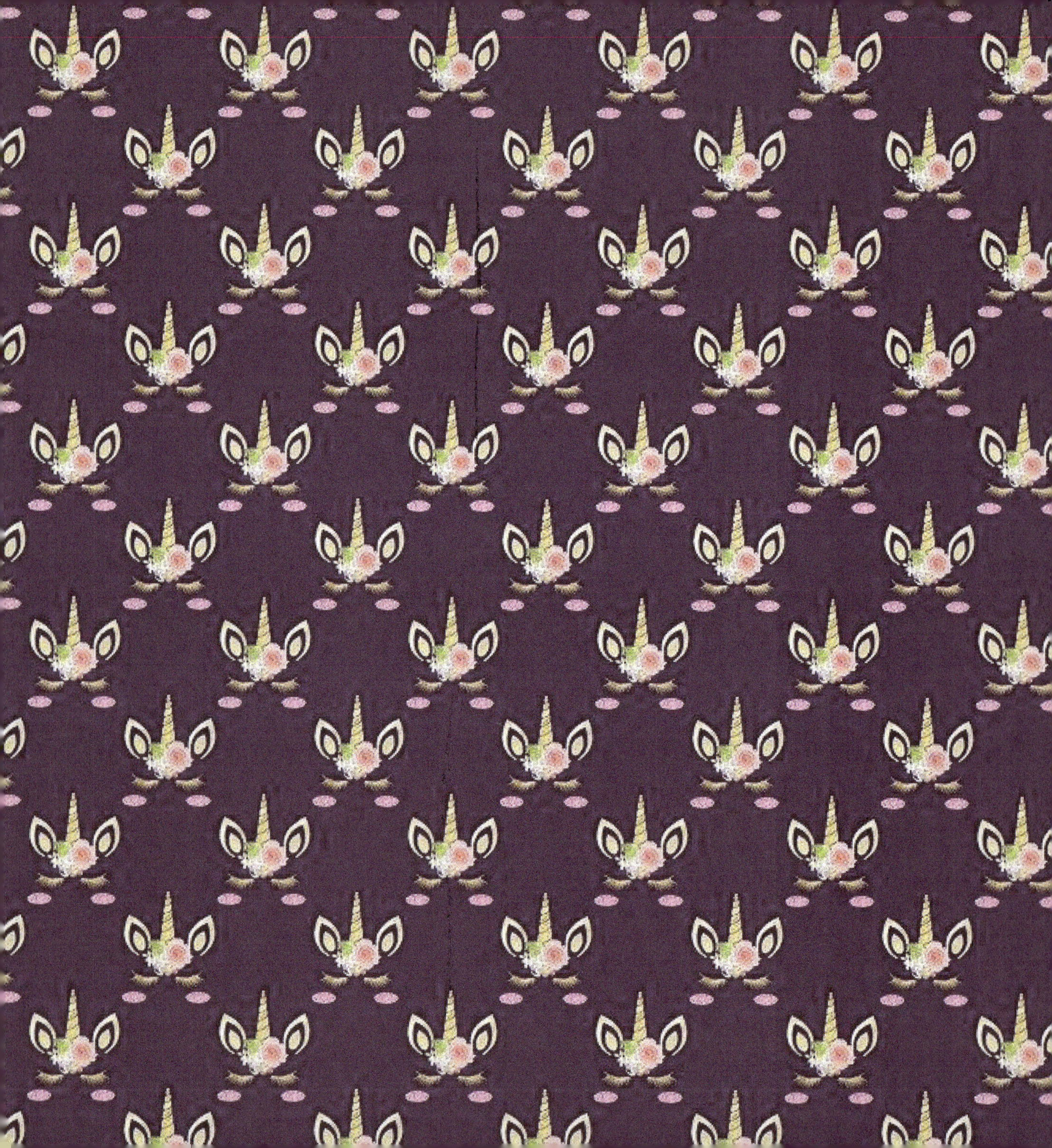

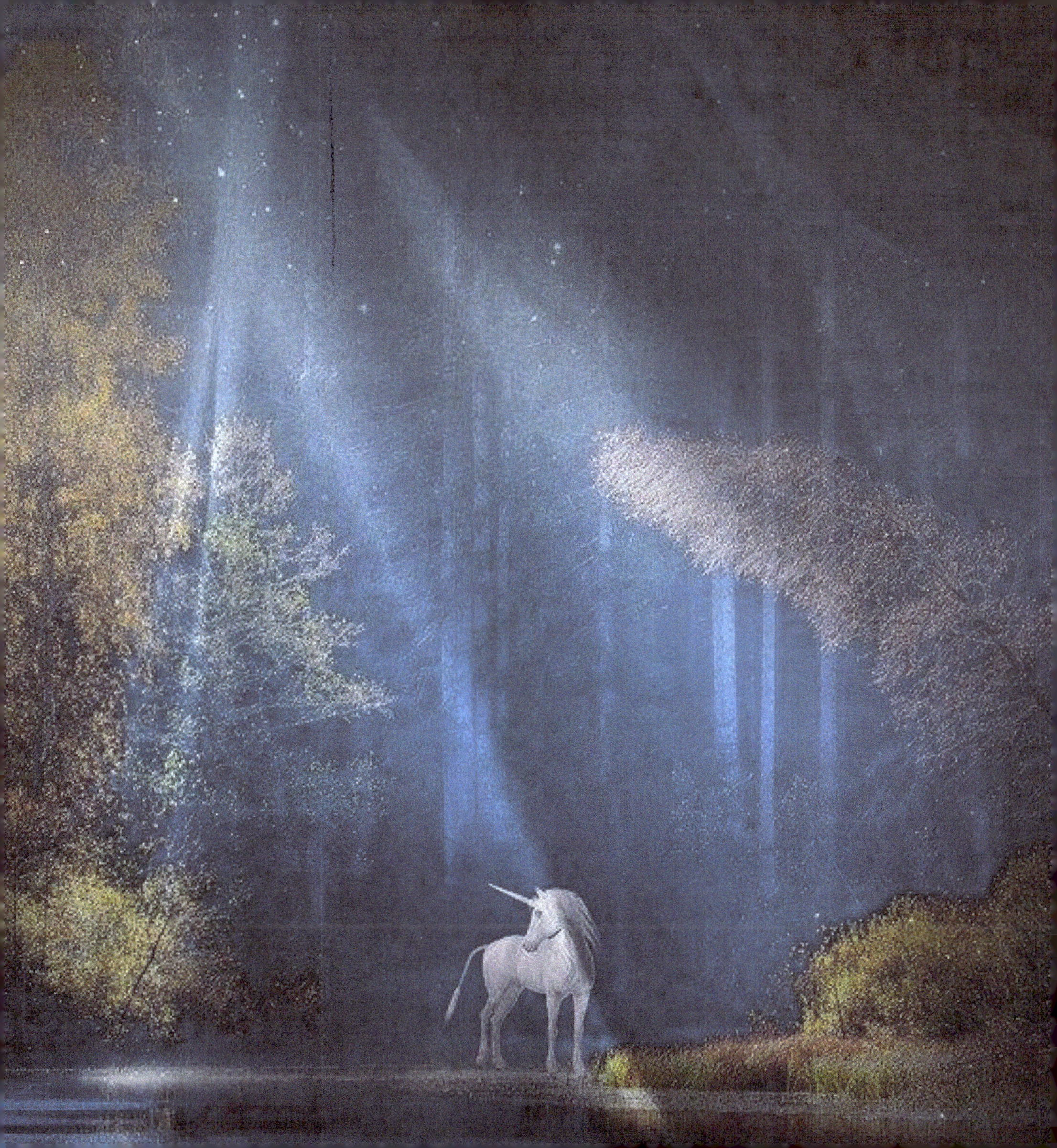

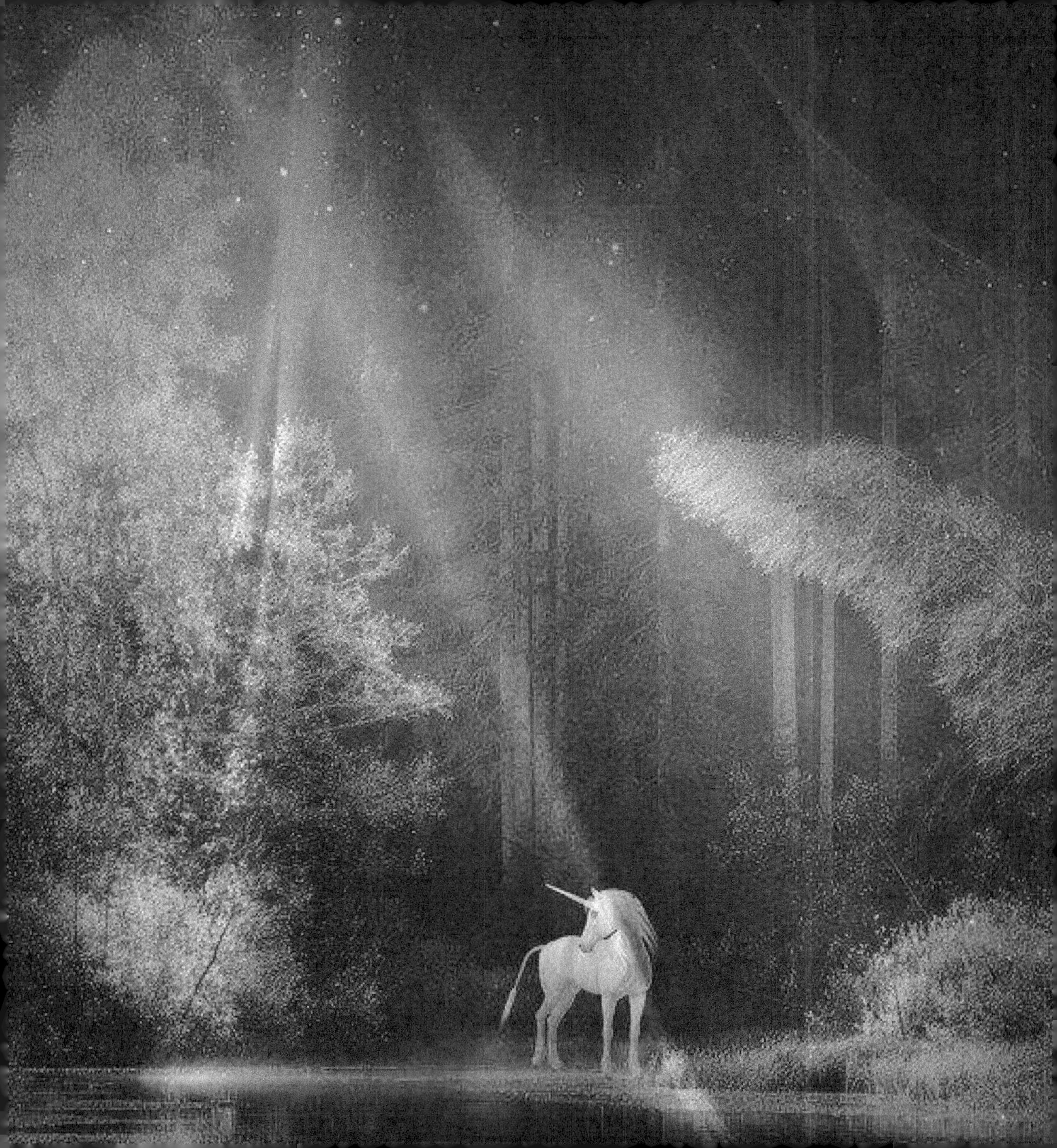

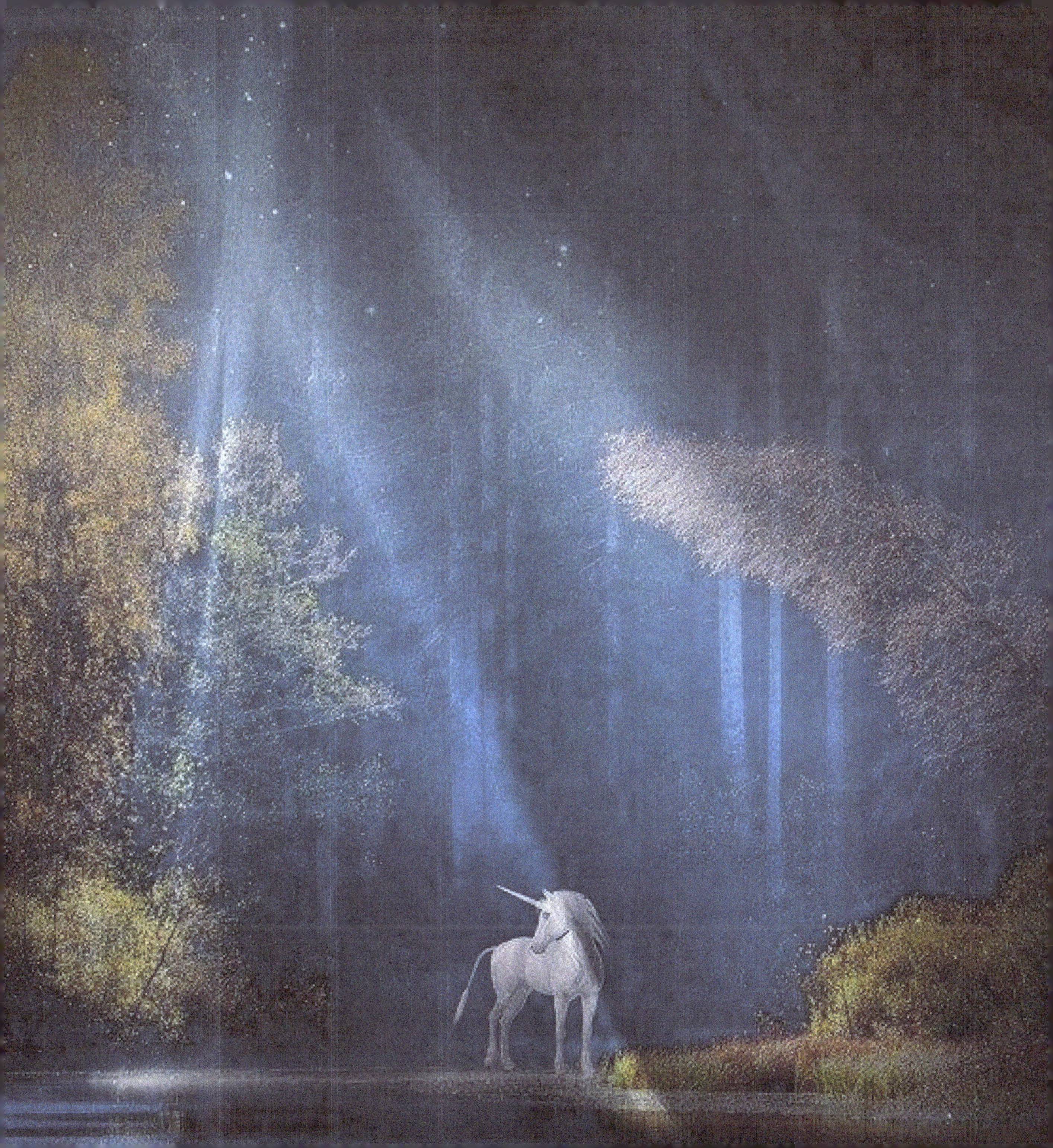

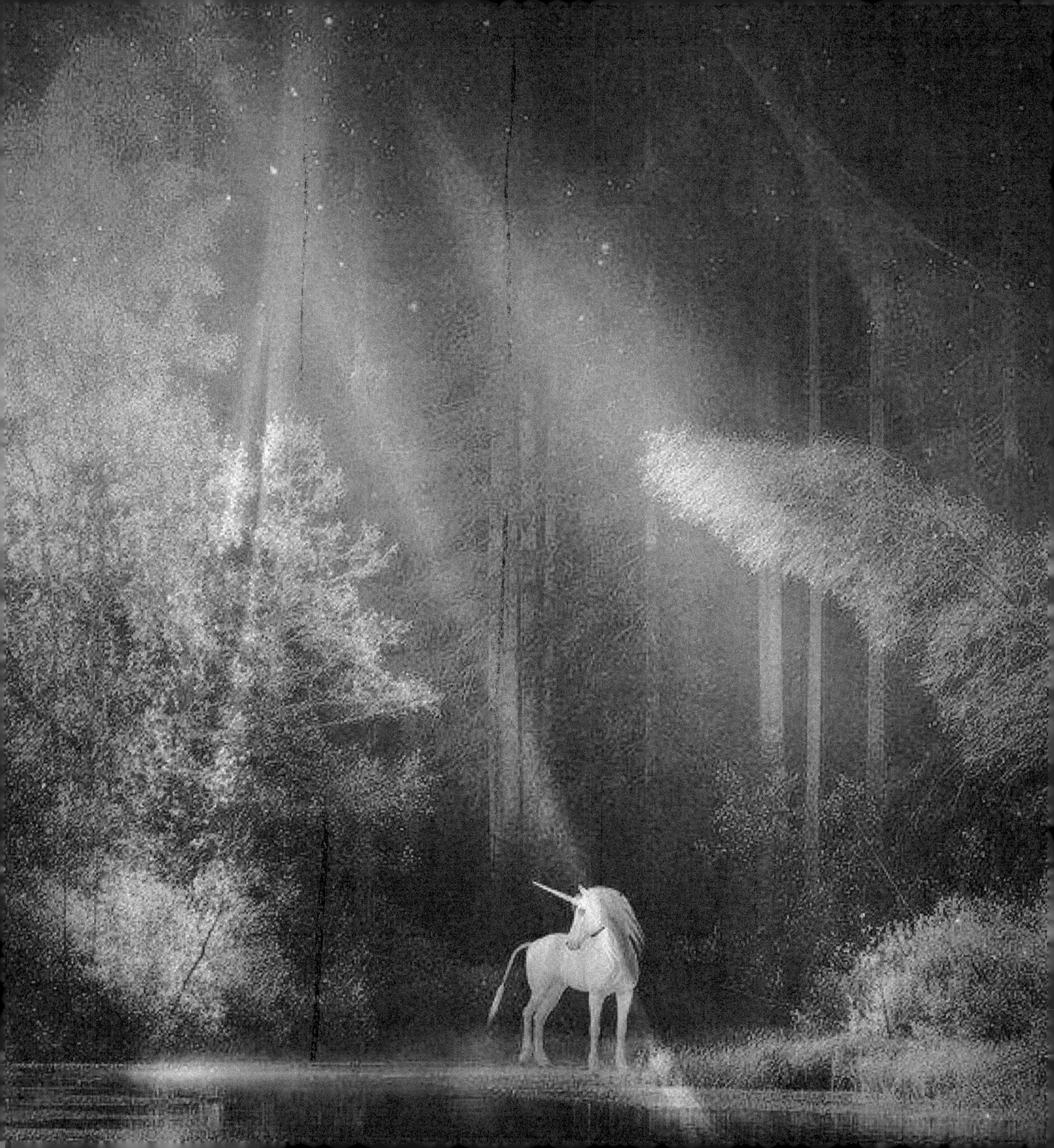

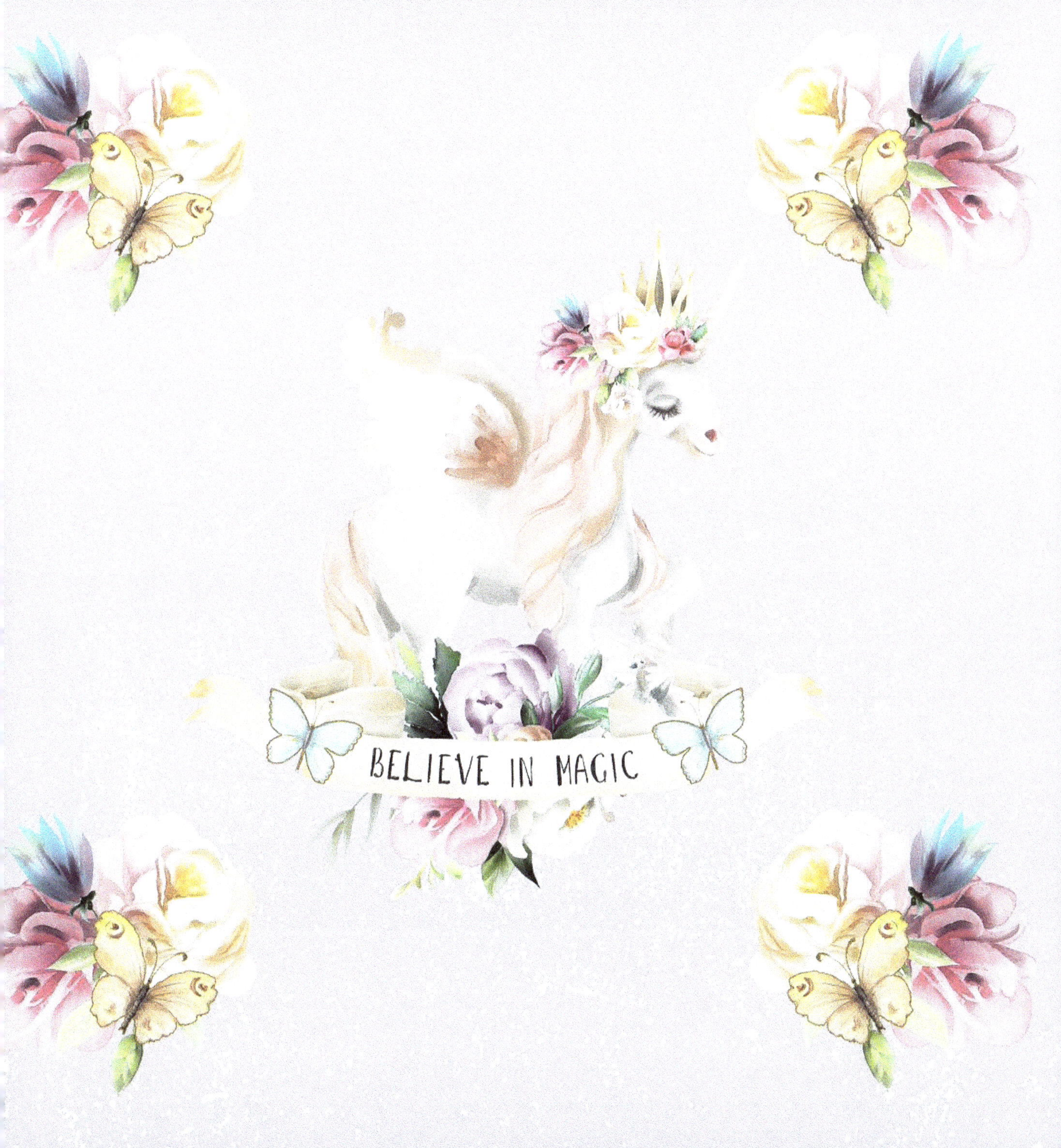
BELIEVE IN MAGIC

BELIEVE IN MAGIC

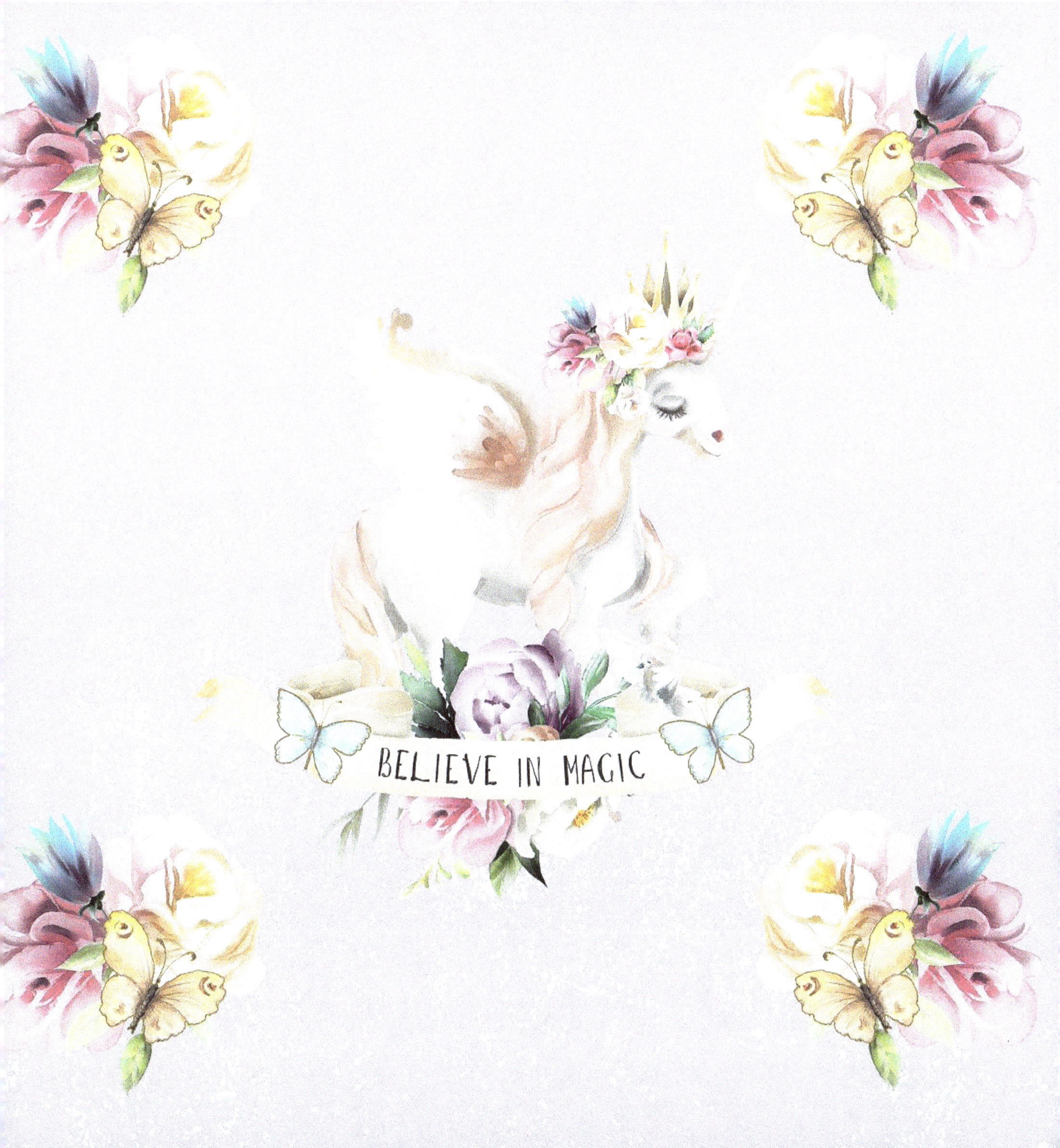
BELIEVE IN MAGIC

BELIEVE IN MAGIC

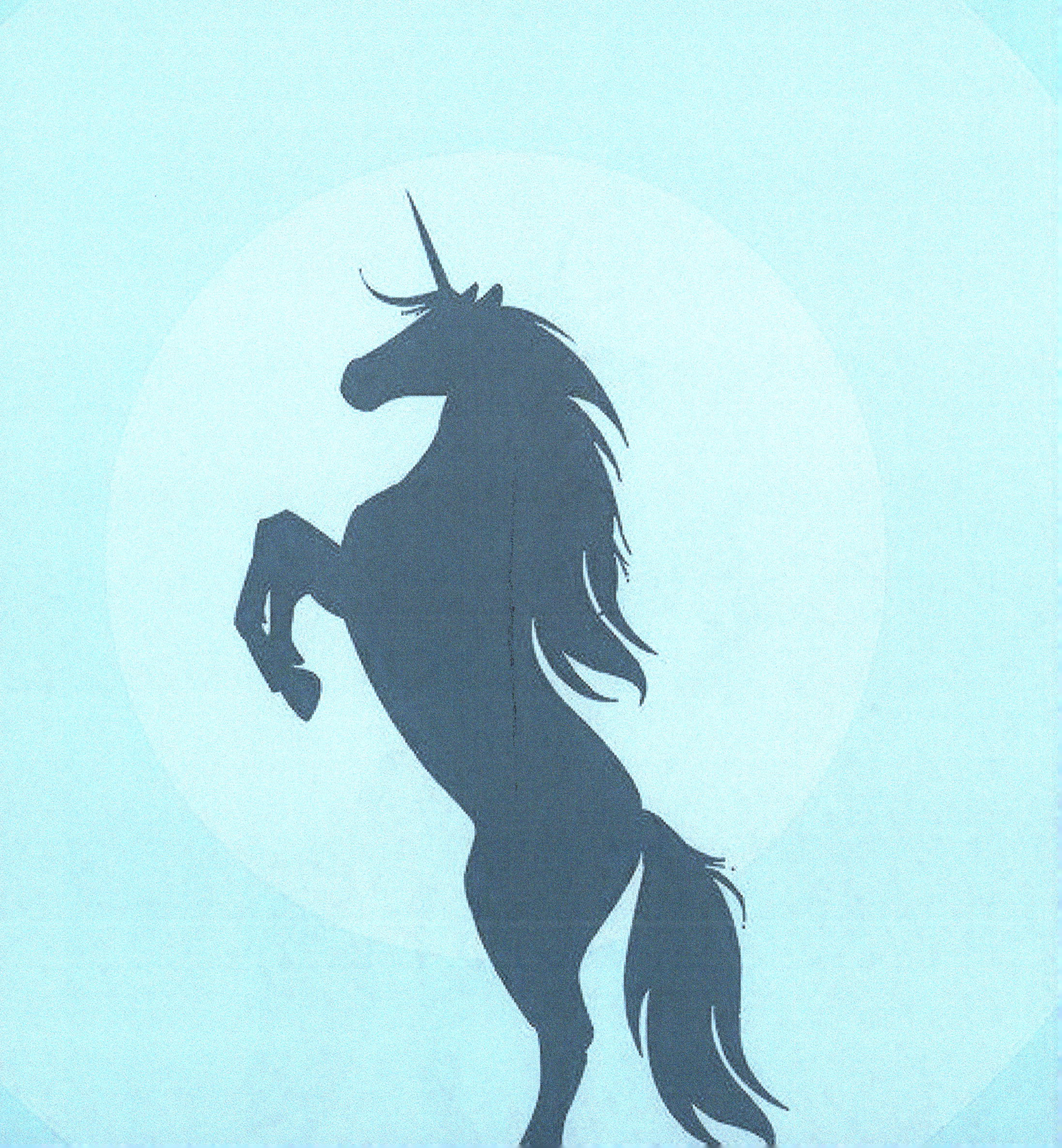

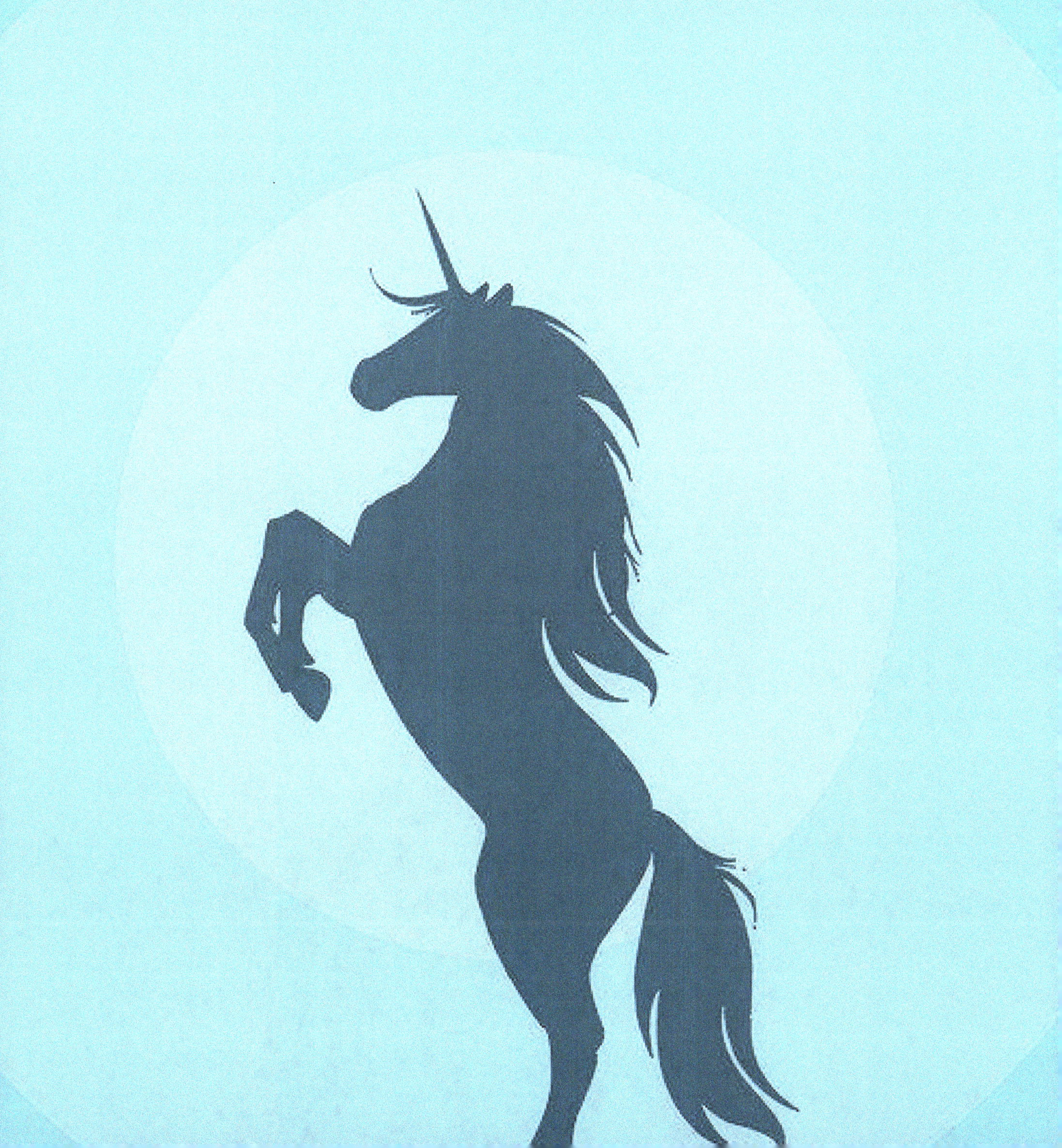

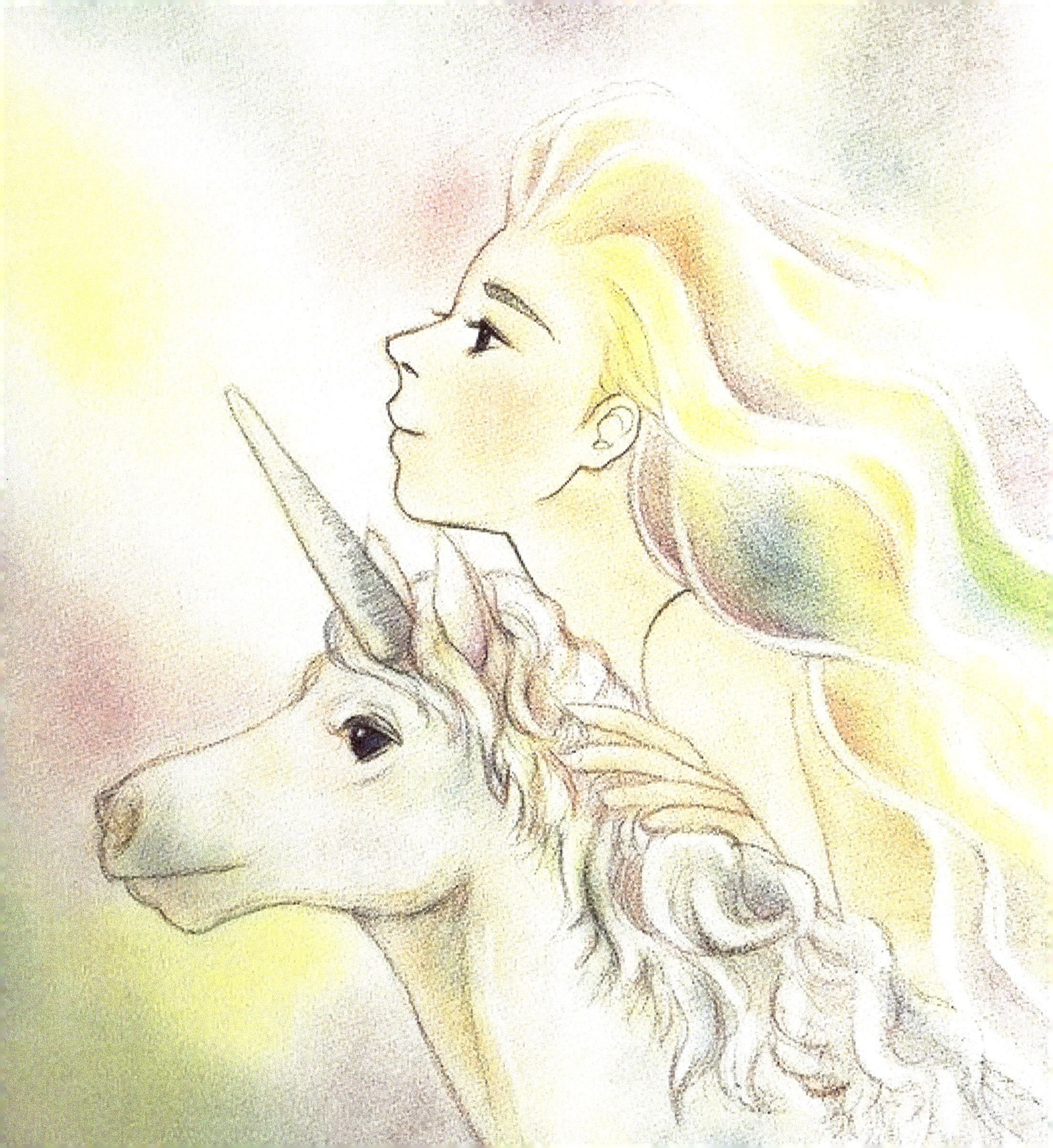

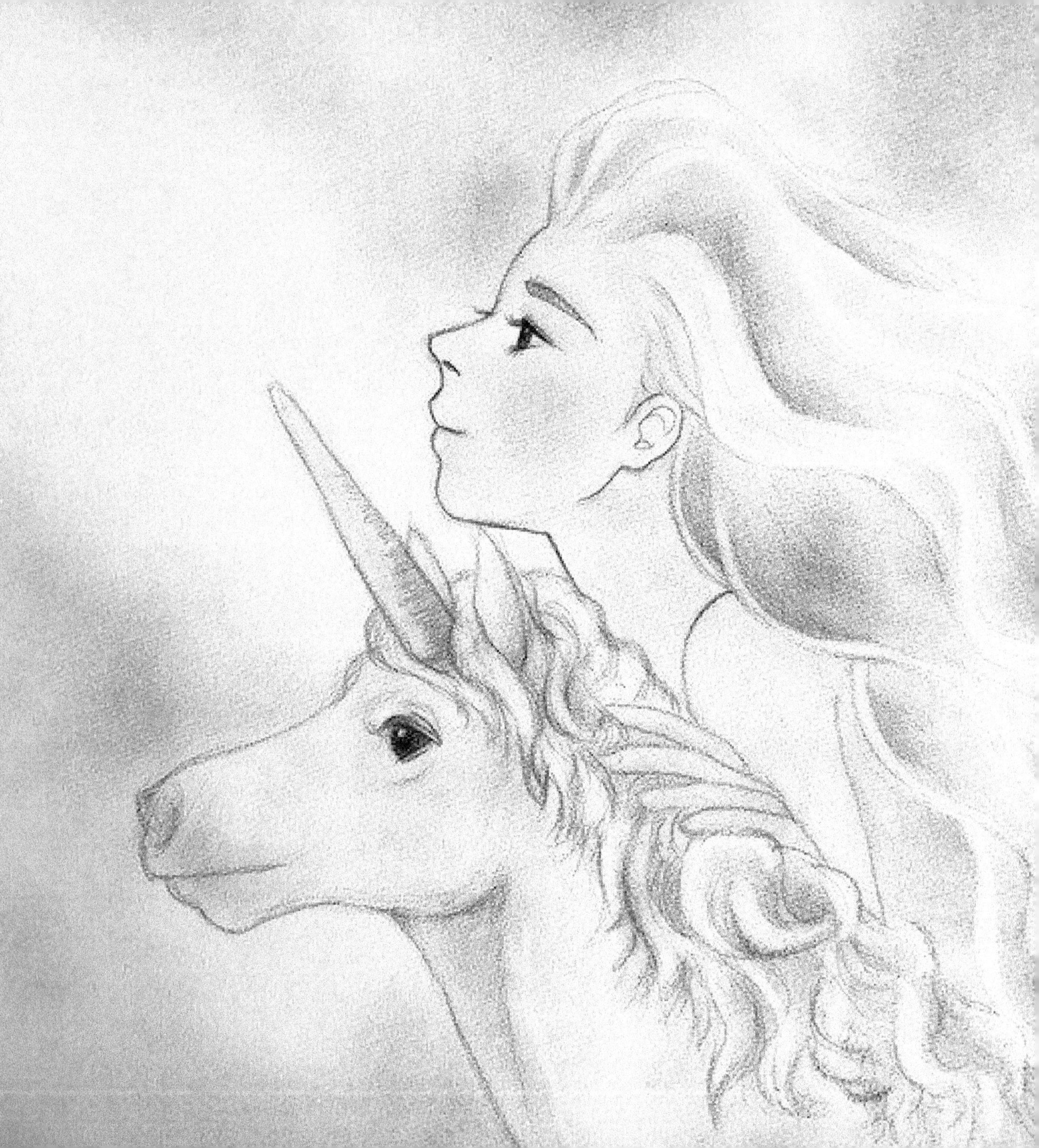

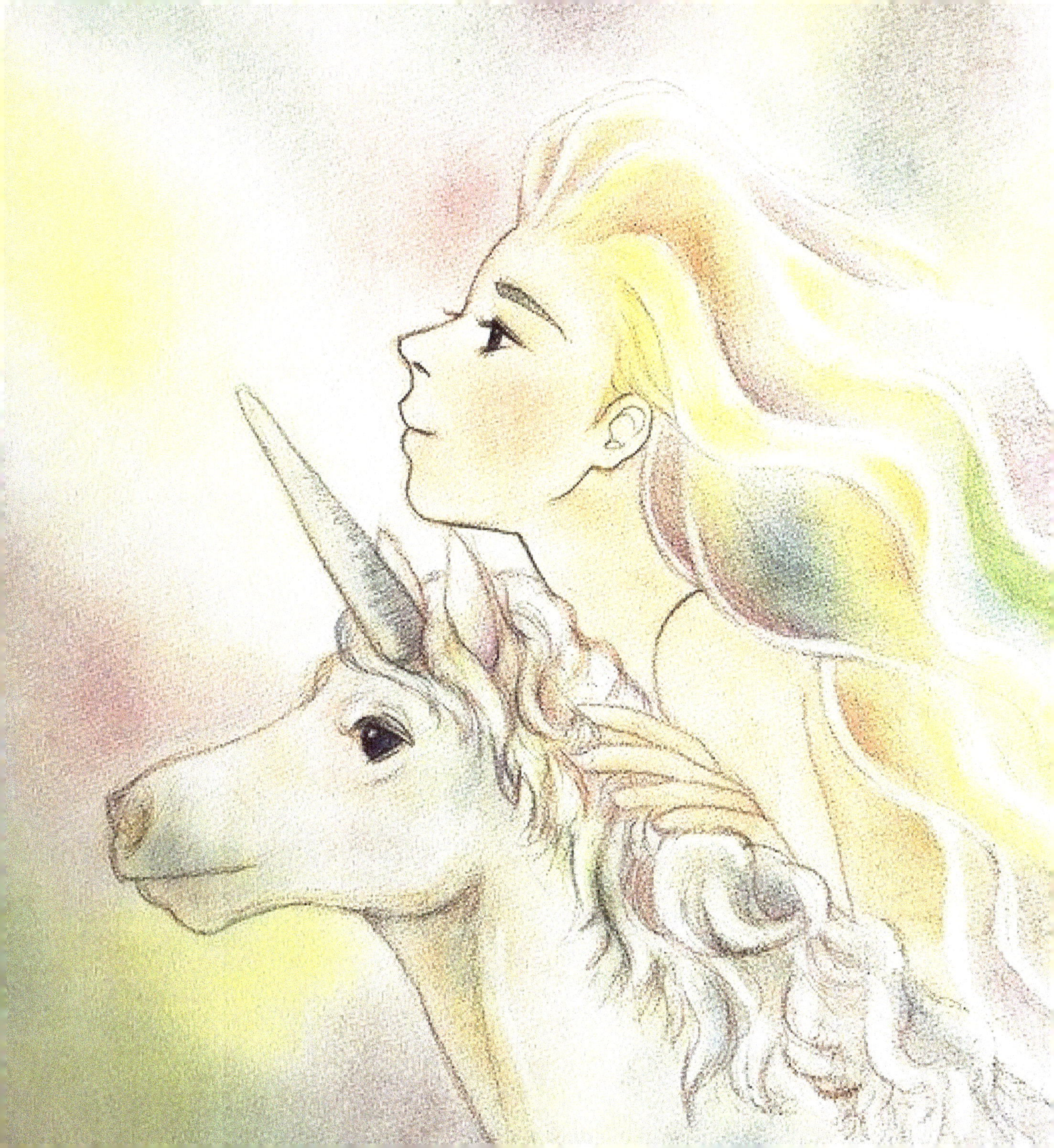

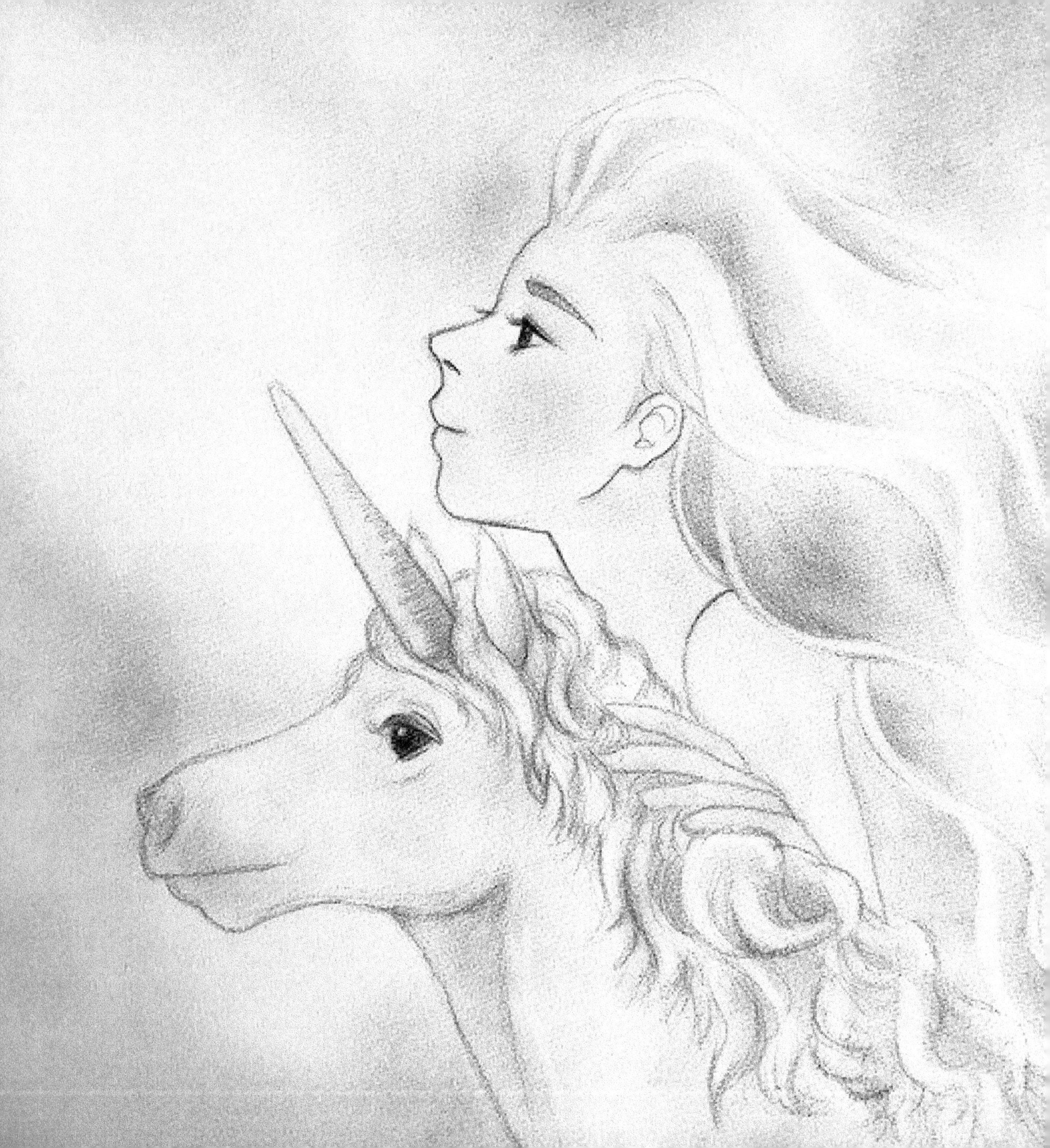